Chord/Melody Solos
for Jazz Guitar

Arranged by Paul Pappas

CONTENTS

Cherry Lane Music
Director of Publications/Project Editor: Mark Phillips
ISBN 1-57560-702-6

Visit our website at www.cherrylane.com

Be Careful, It's My Heart

from HOLIDAY INN

Words and Music by Irving Berlin

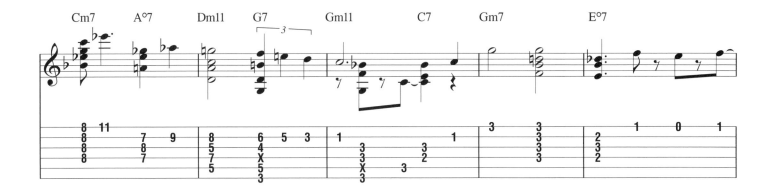

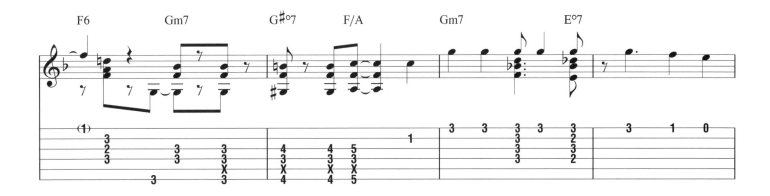

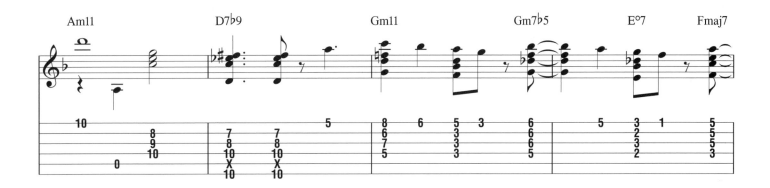

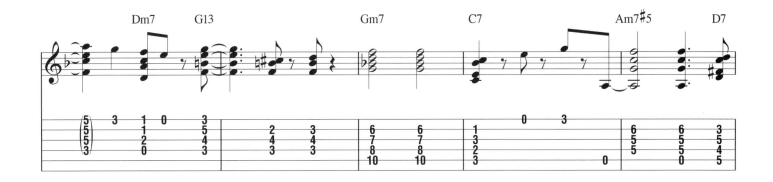

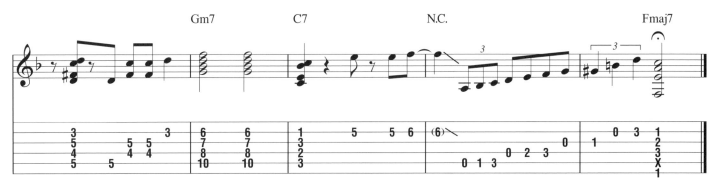

The Blue Room

from THE GIRL FRIEND

Words by Lorenz Hart
Music by Richard Rodgers

Moderate Swing

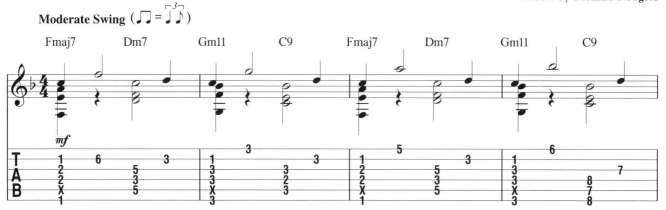

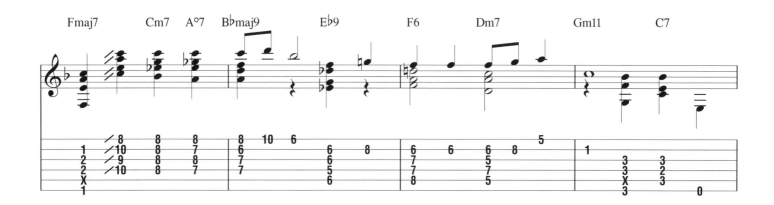

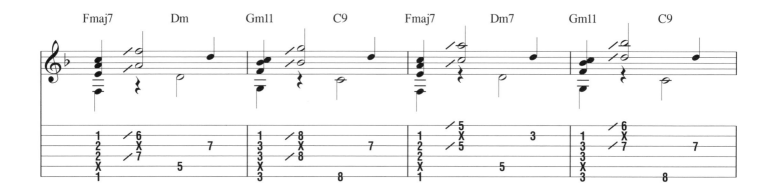

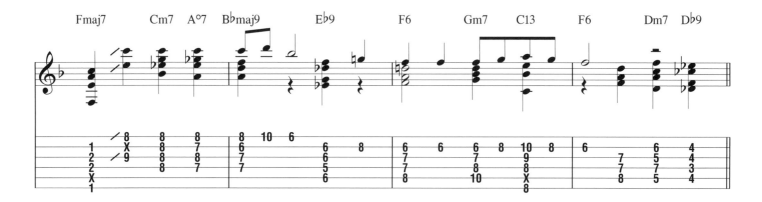

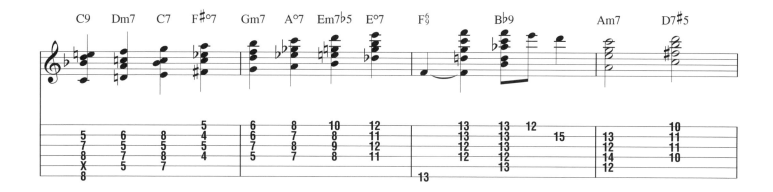

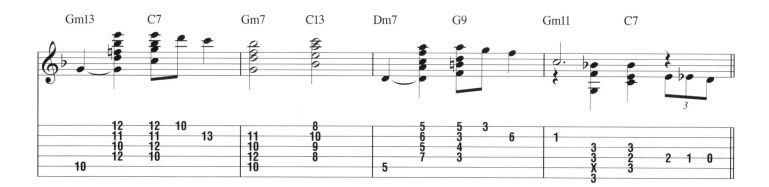

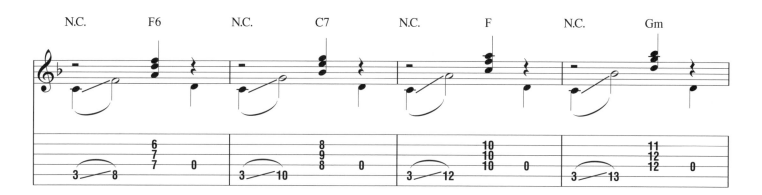

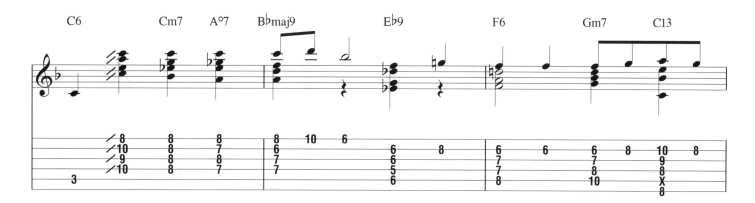

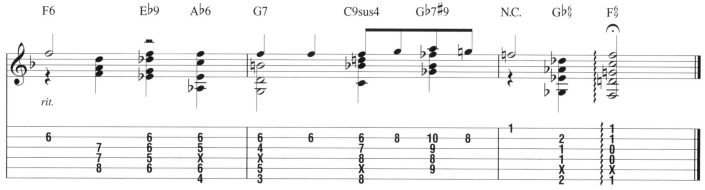

But Beautiful
from ROAD TO RIO

Words by Johnny Burke
Music by Jimmy Van Heusen

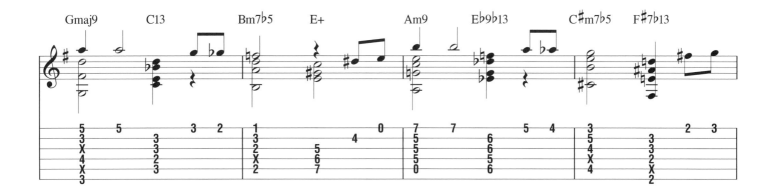

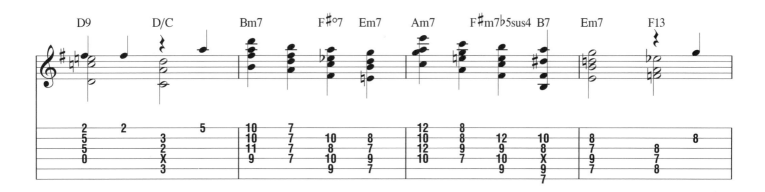

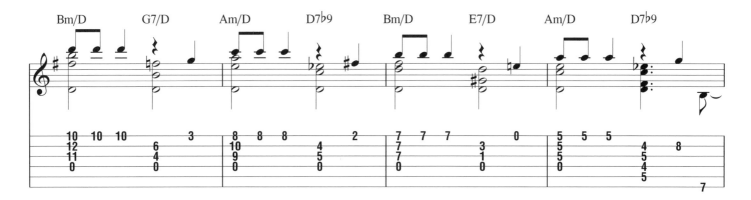

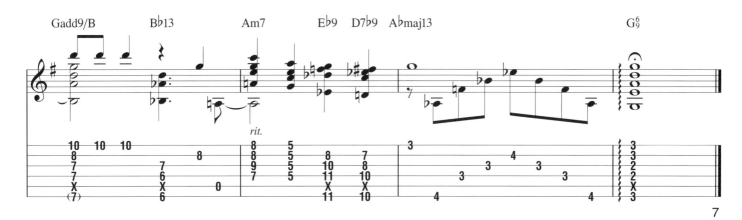

Come Fly with Me

Words by Sammy Cahn
Music by James Van Heusen

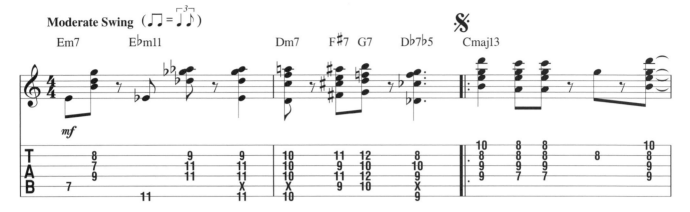

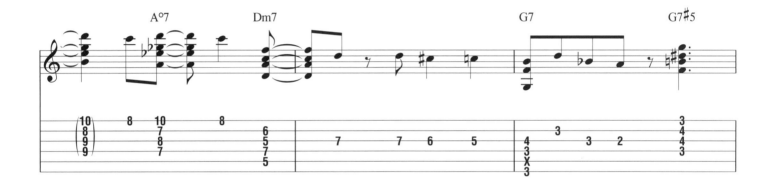

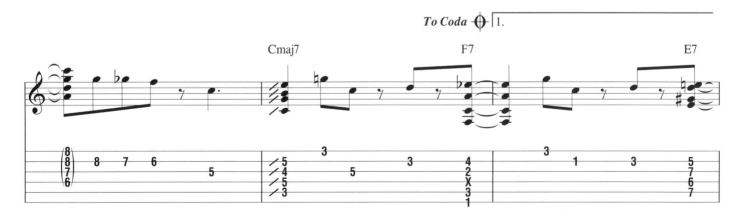

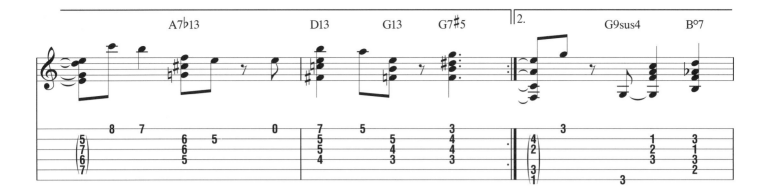

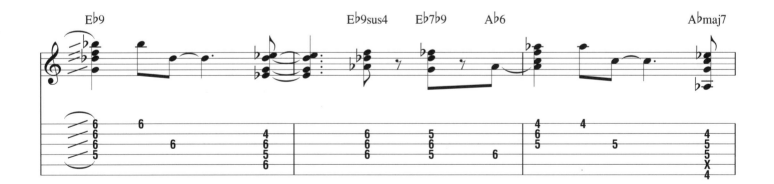

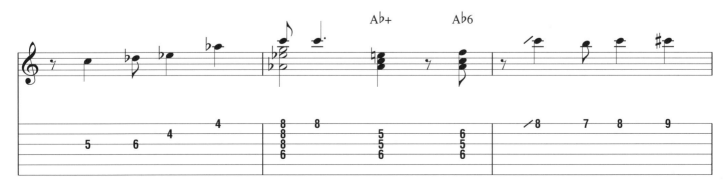

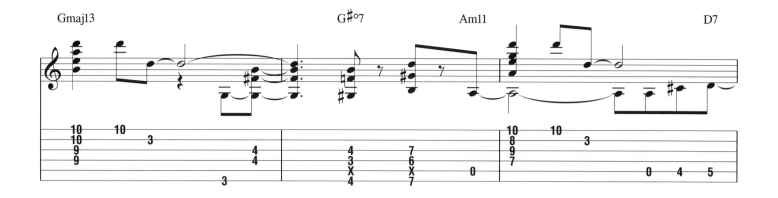

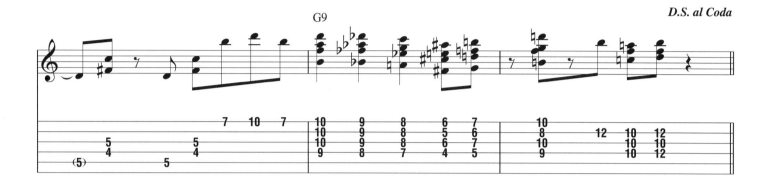

D.S. al Coda

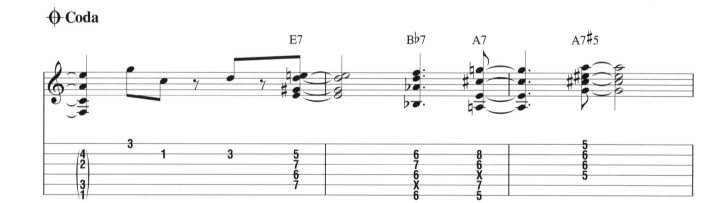

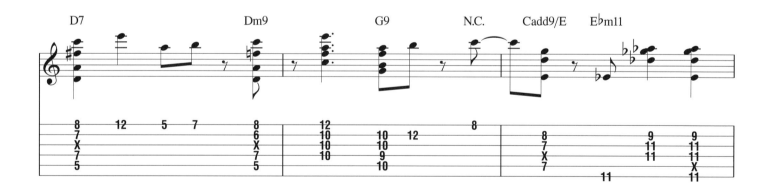

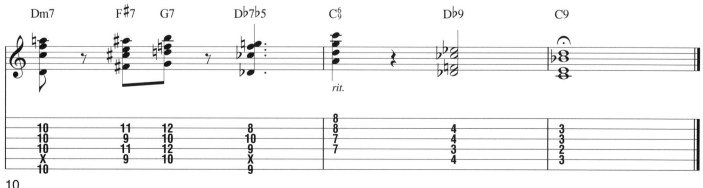

Here's That Rainy Day
from CARNIVAL IN FLANDERS

Words by Johnny Burke
Music by Jimmy Van Heusen

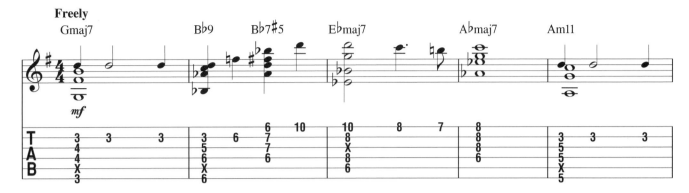

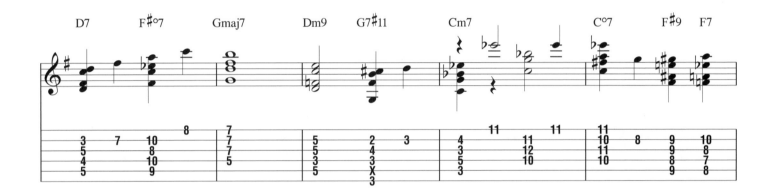

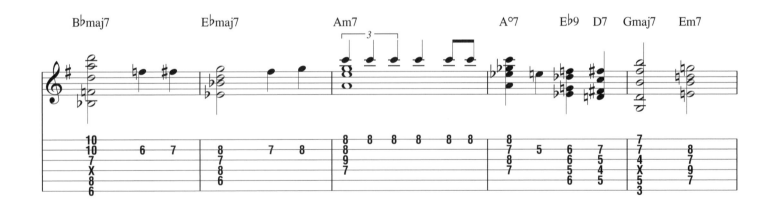

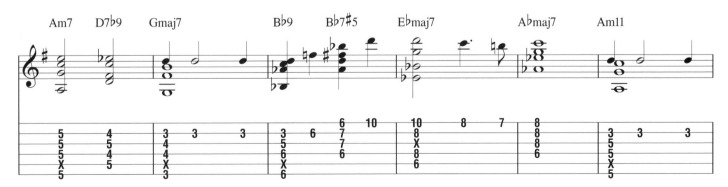

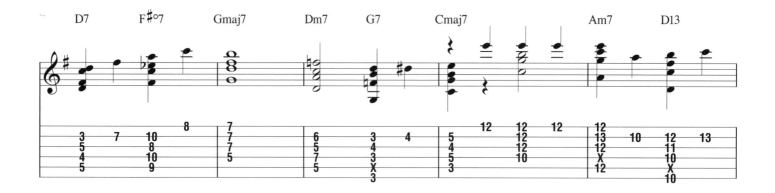

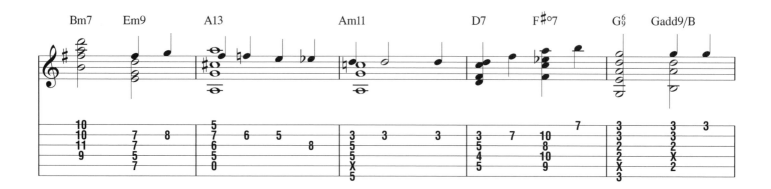

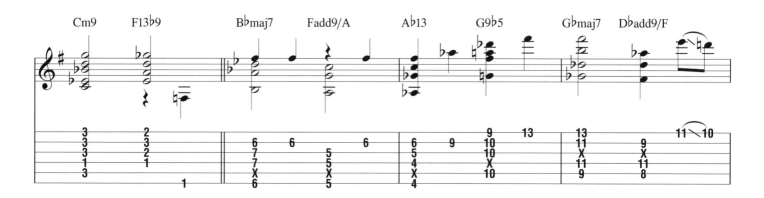

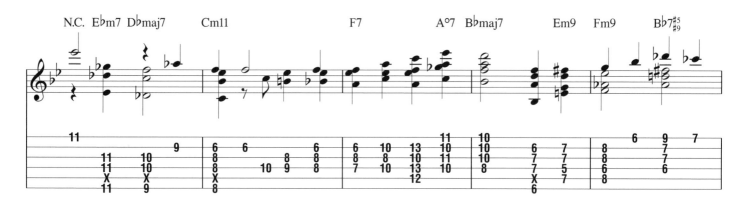

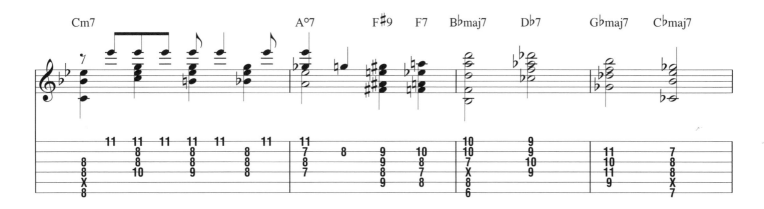

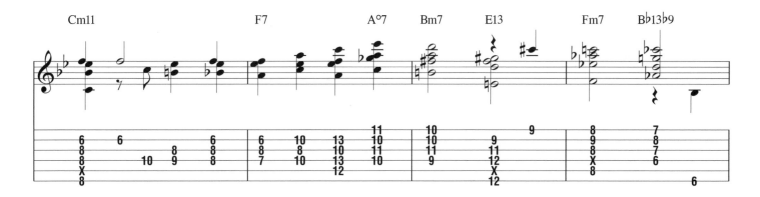

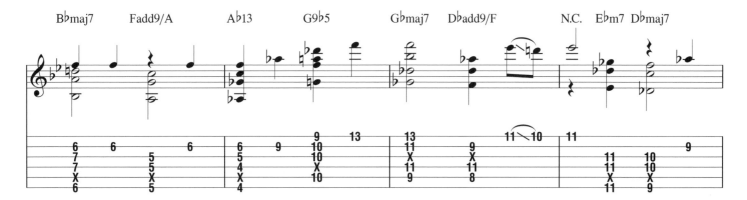

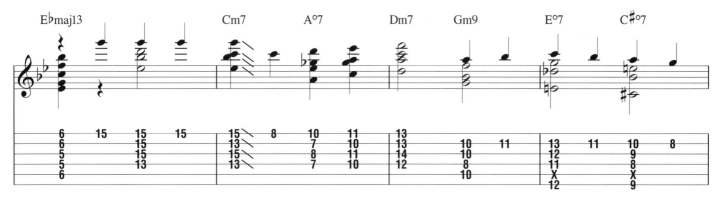

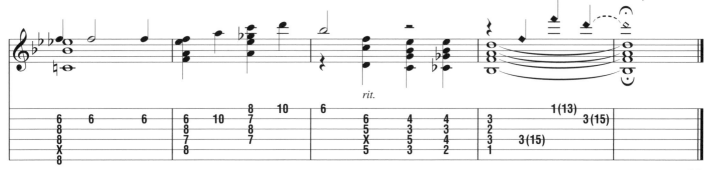

Fly Me to the Moon
(In Other Words)
featured in the Motion Picture ONCE AROUND

Words and Music by Bart Howard

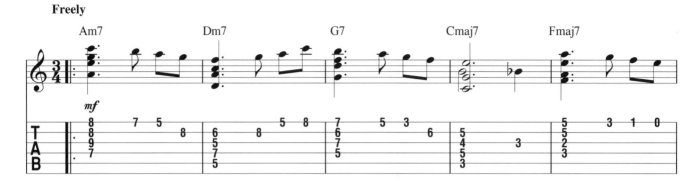

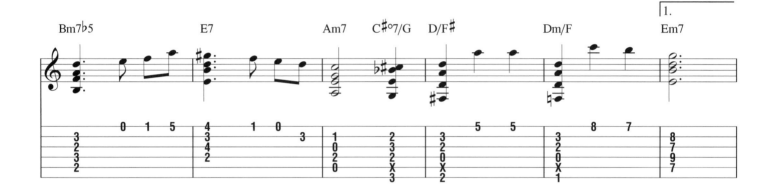

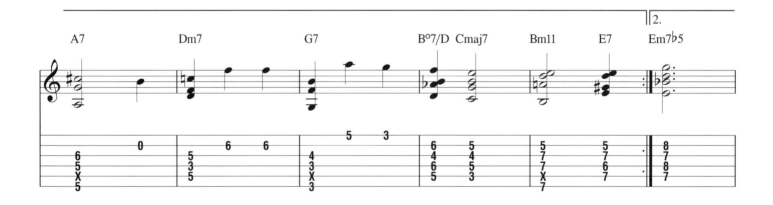

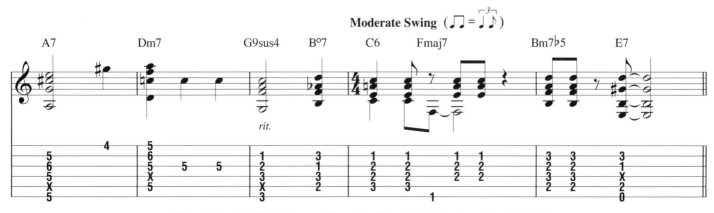

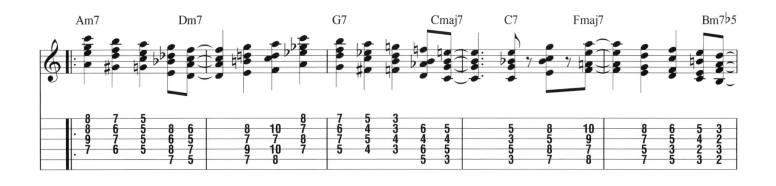

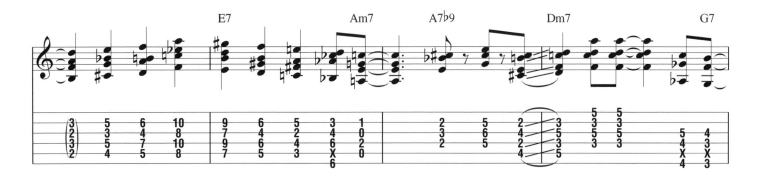

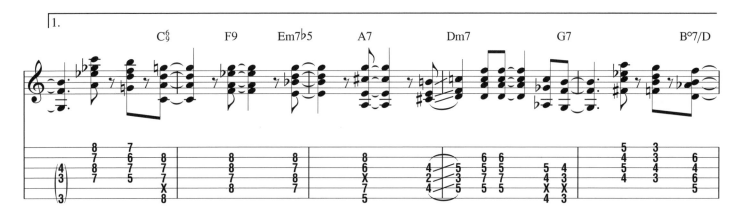

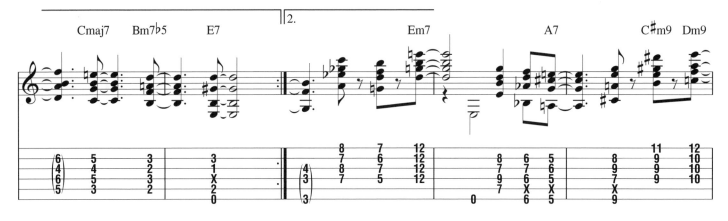

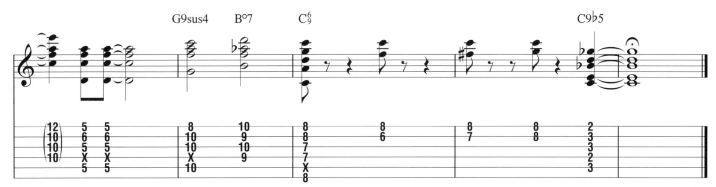

I Can't Get Started with You

from ZIEGFELD FOLLIES

Words by Ira Gershwin
Music by Vernon Duke

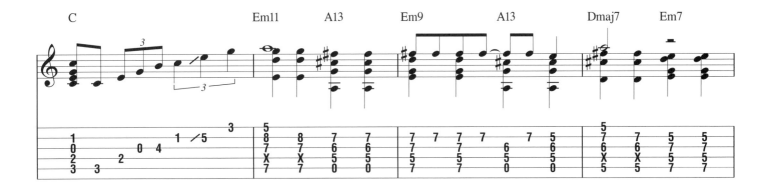

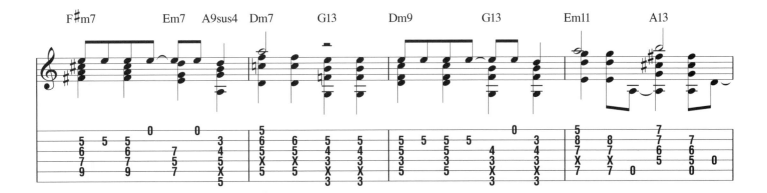

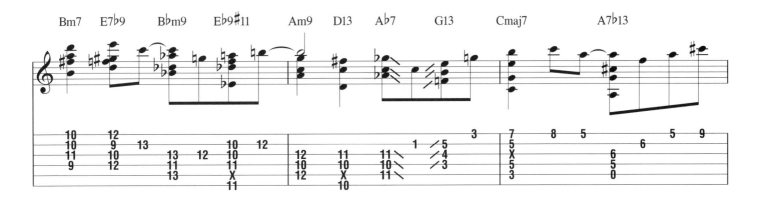

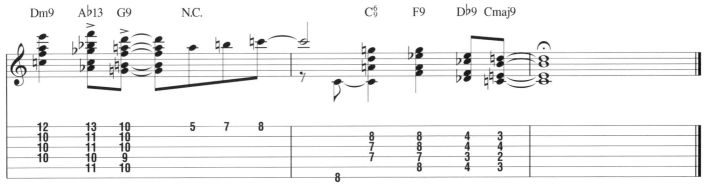

I've Got the World on a String

Lyric by Ted Koehler
Music by Harold Arlen

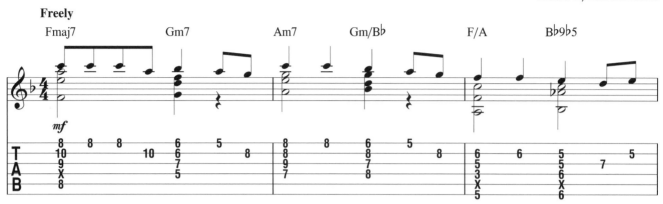

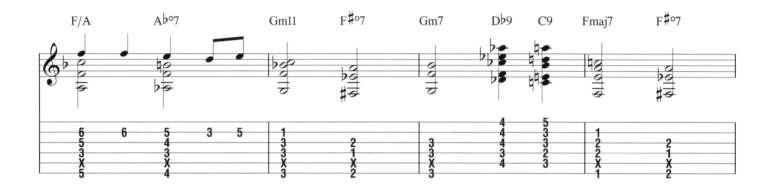

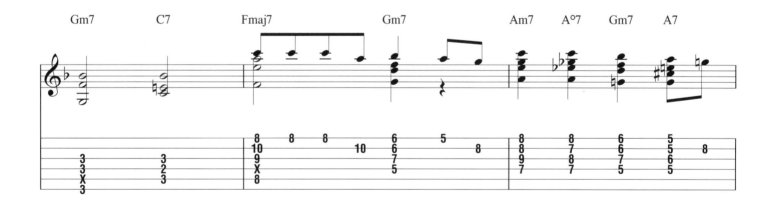

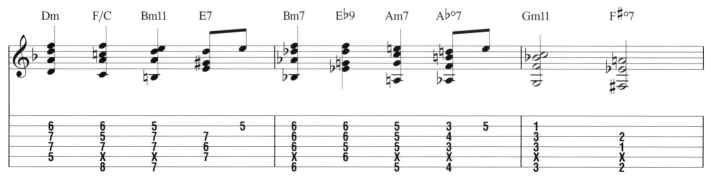

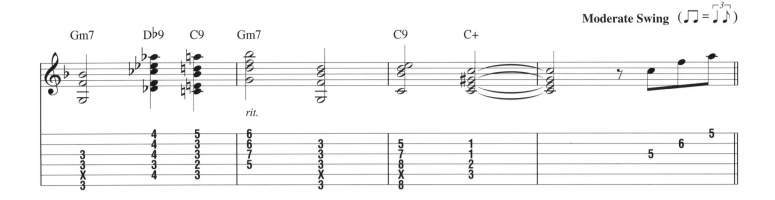

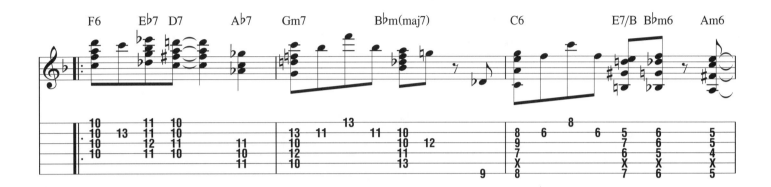

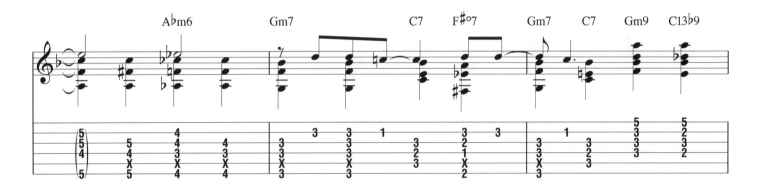

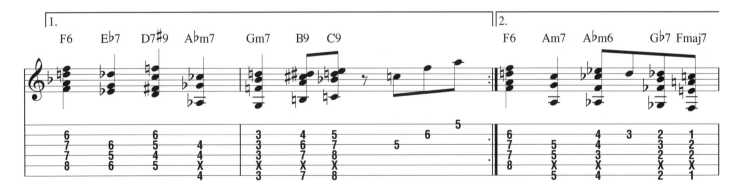

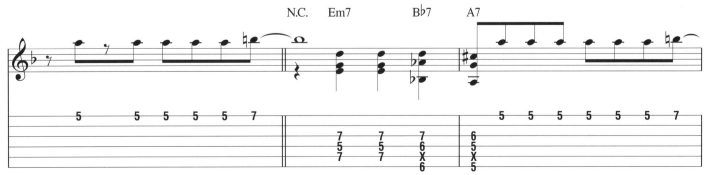

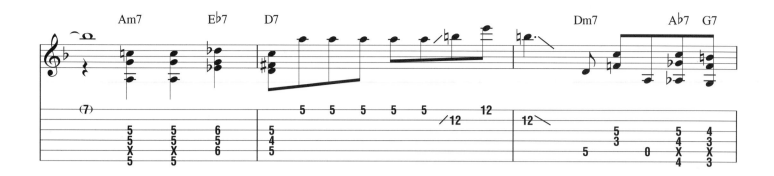

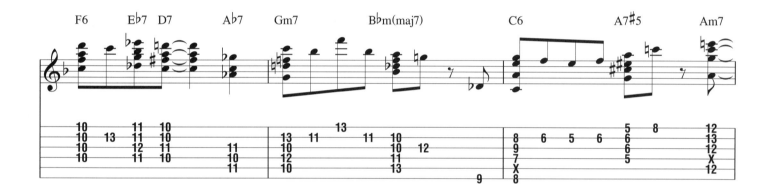

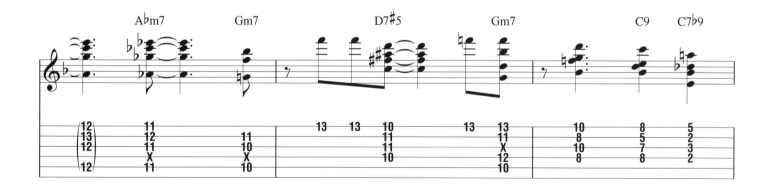

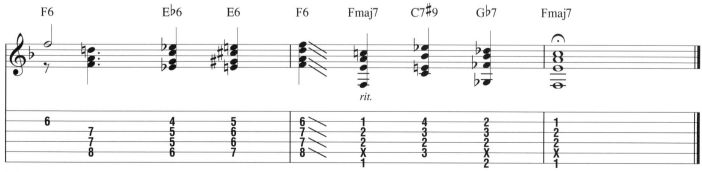

Just the Two of Us

Words and Music by Ralph MacDonald,
William Salter and Bill Withers

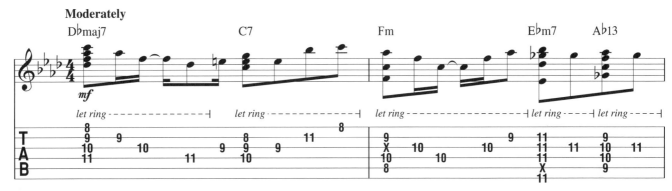

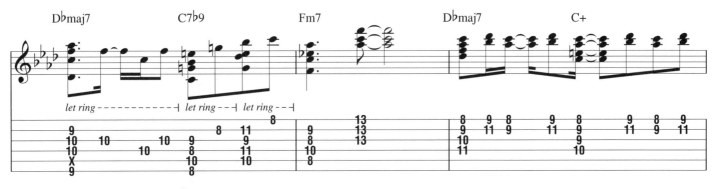

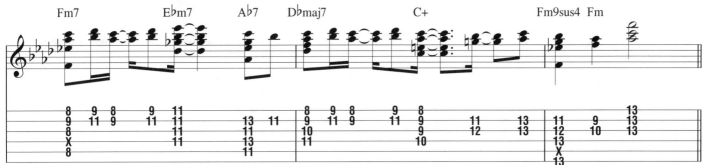

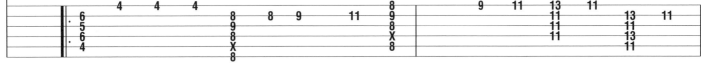

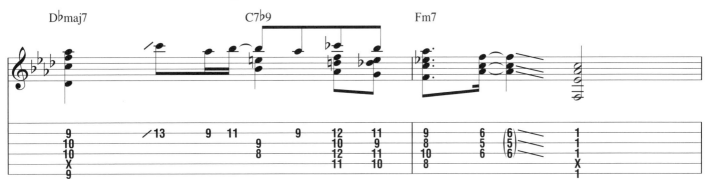

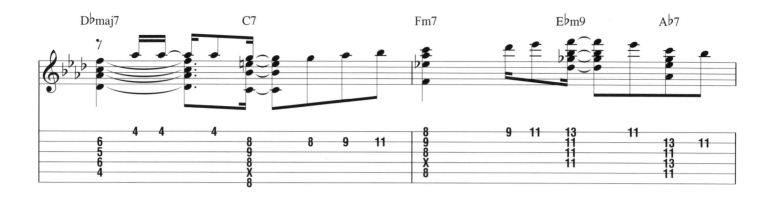

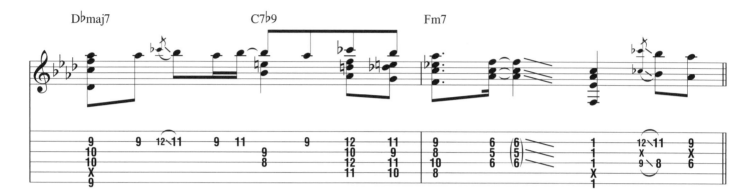

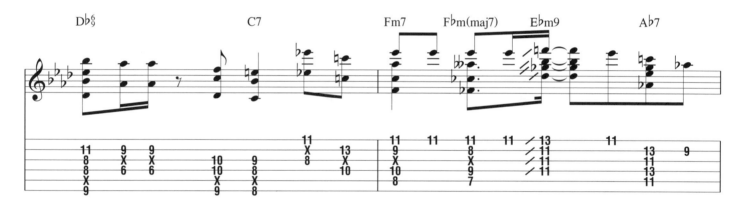

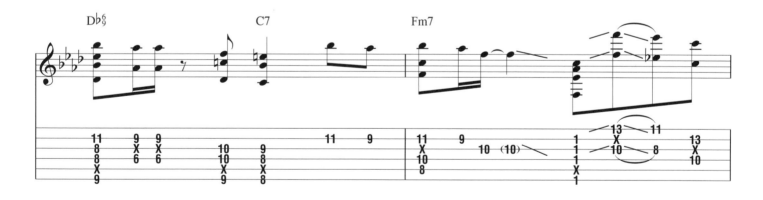

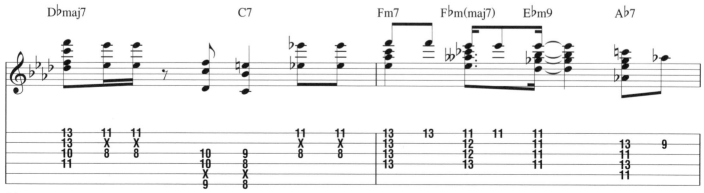

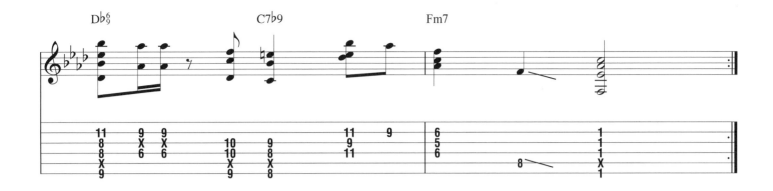

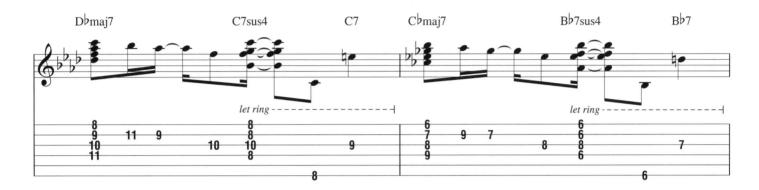

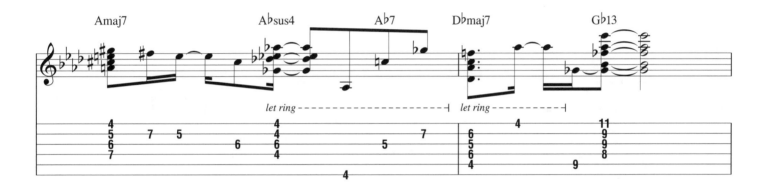

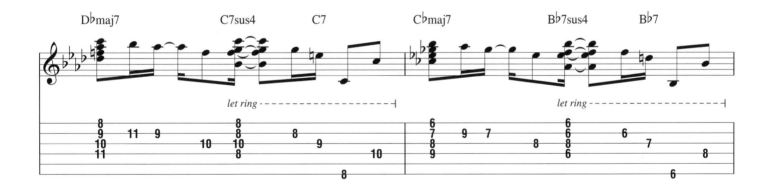

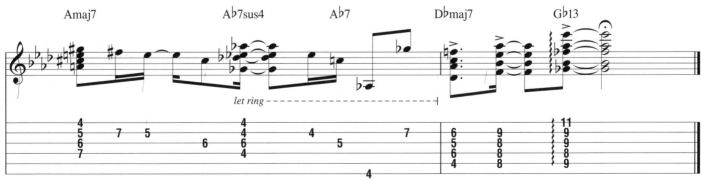

It Never Entered My Mind

from HIGHER AND HIGHER

Words by Lorenz Hart
Music by Richard Rodgers

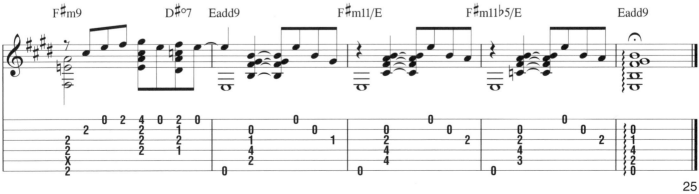

Misty

Medium Ballad (♫ = ♩♪³)

Music by Erroll Garner

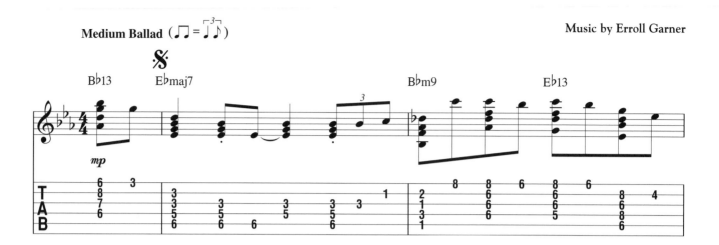

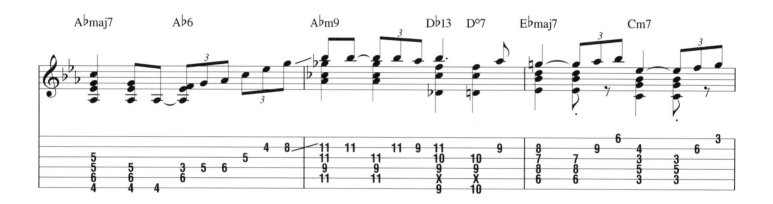

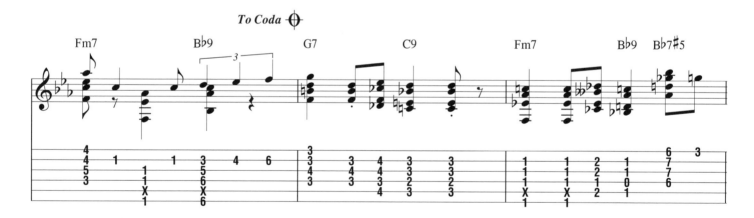

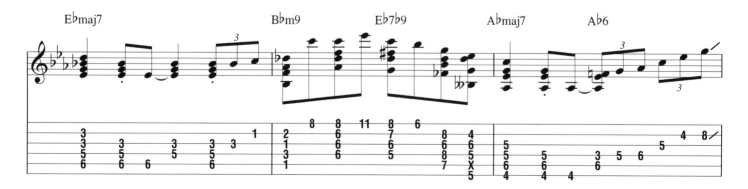

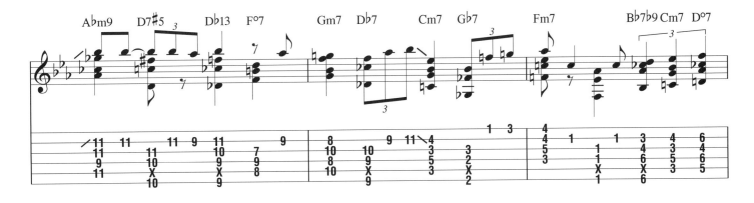

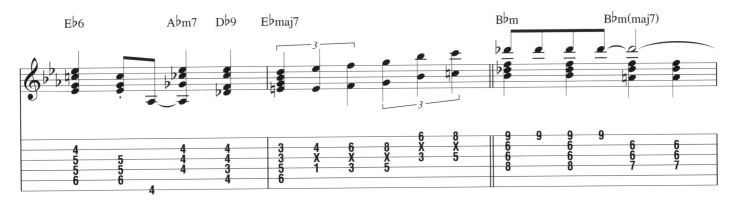

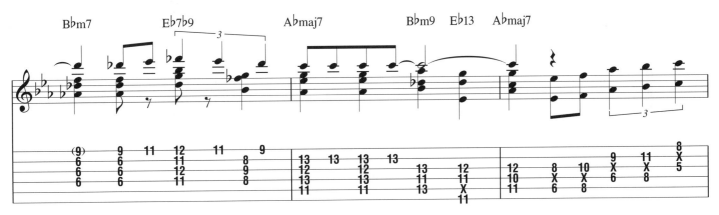

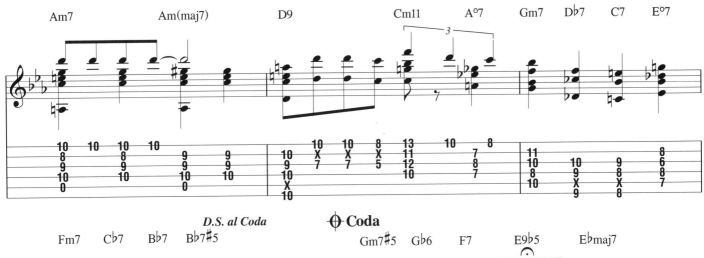

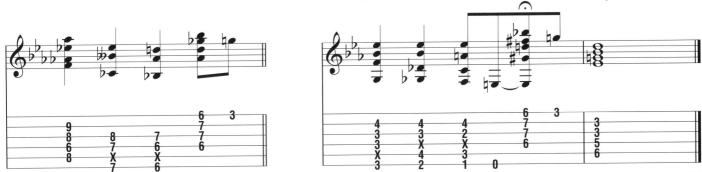

Spring Will Be a Little Late This Year

from the Motion Picture CHRISTMAS HOLIDAY

By Frank Loesser

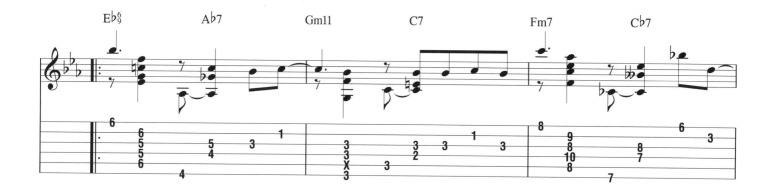

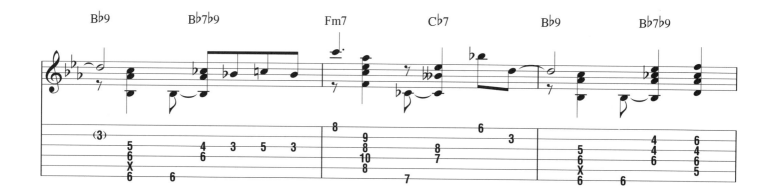

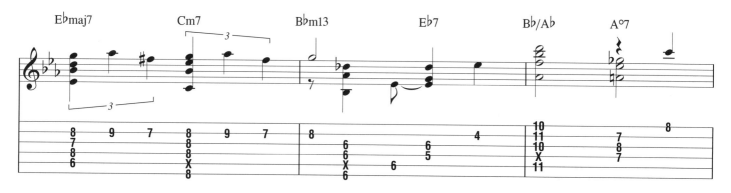

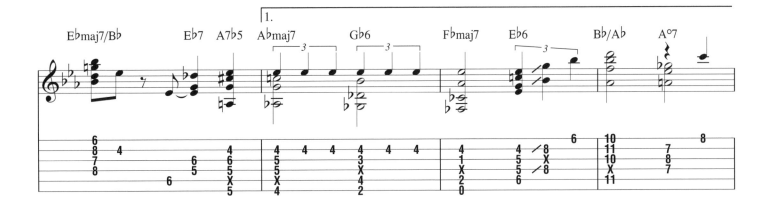

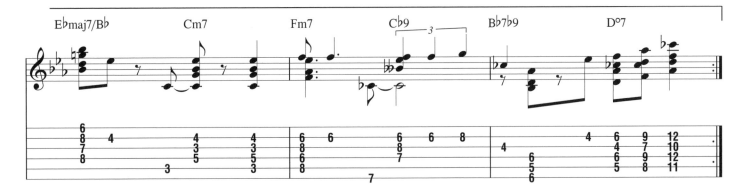

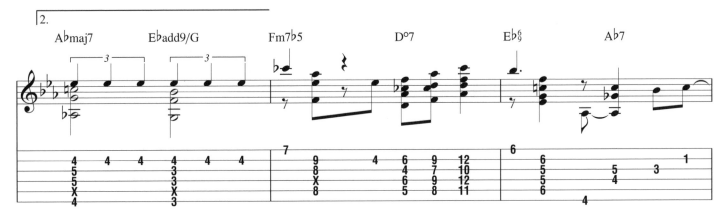

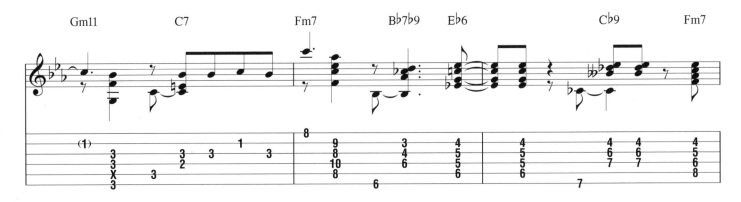

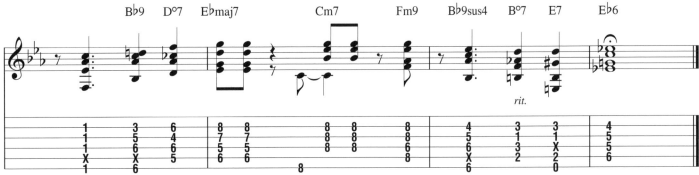

Something to Live For

Words and Music by
Duke Ellington and Billy Strayhorn

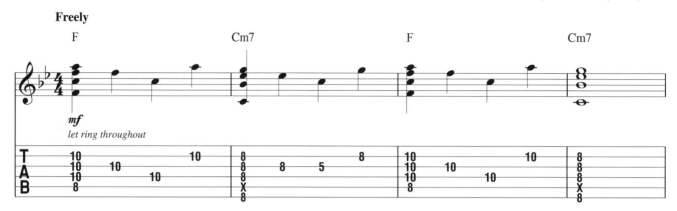

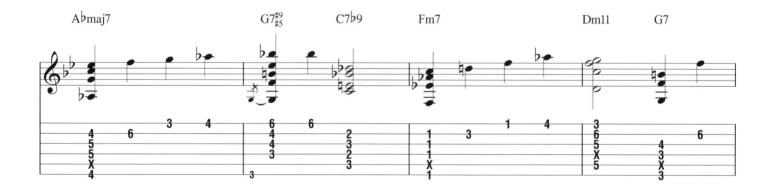

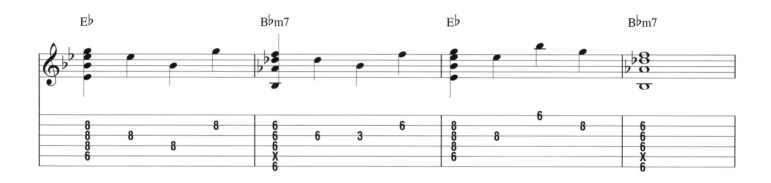

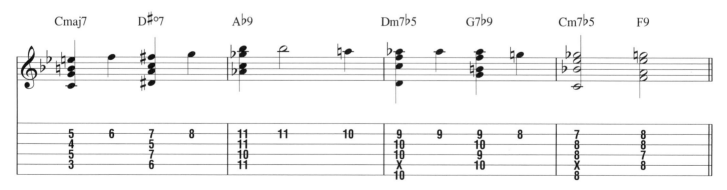

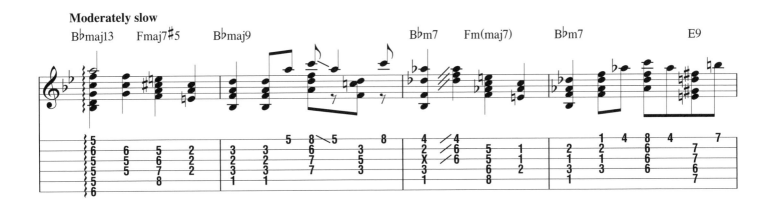

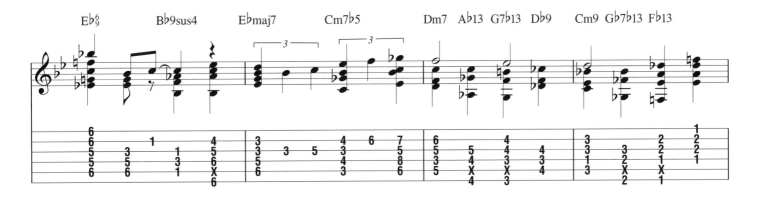

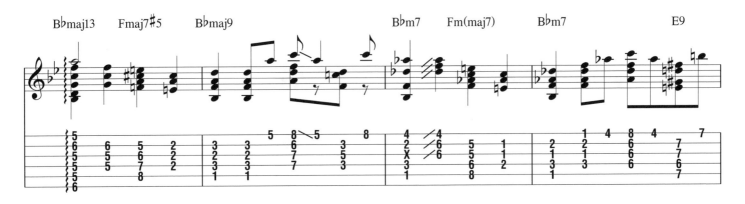

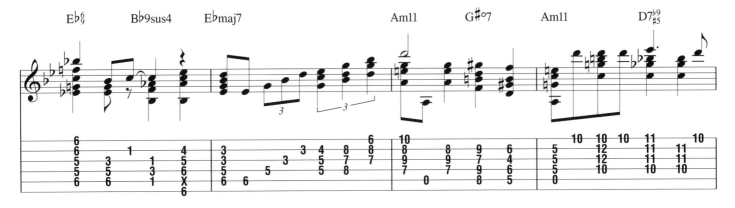

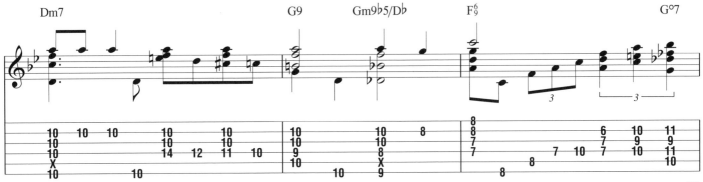

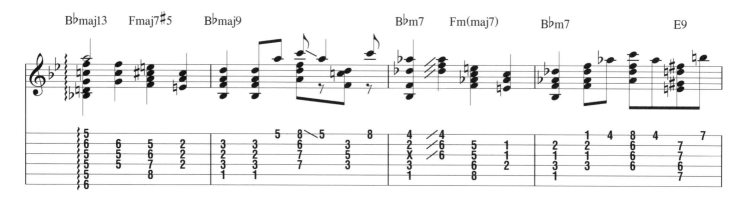

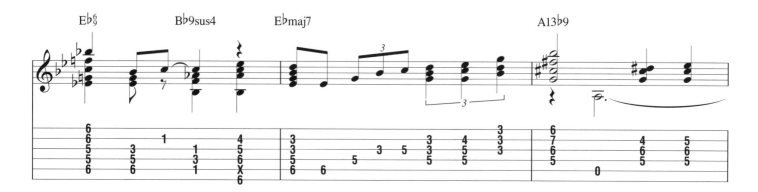

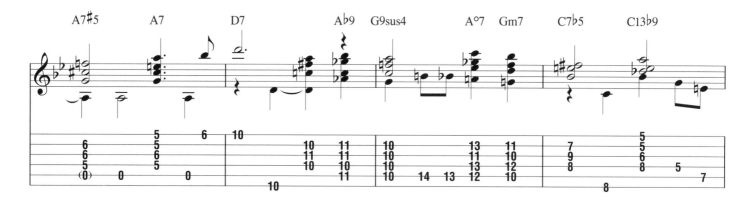

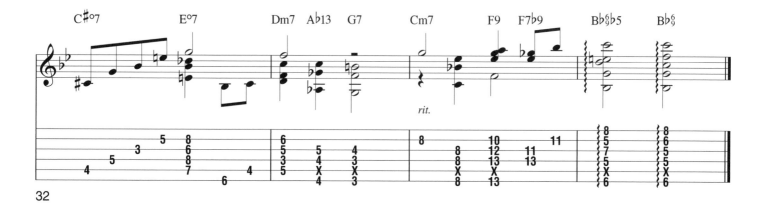

Take the "A" Train

Words and Music by Billy Strayhorn

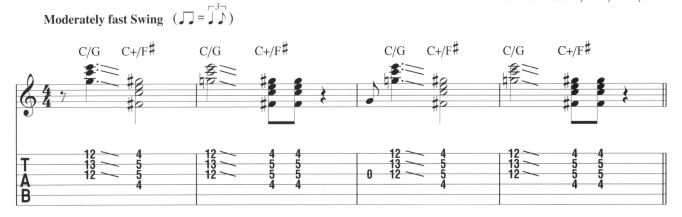

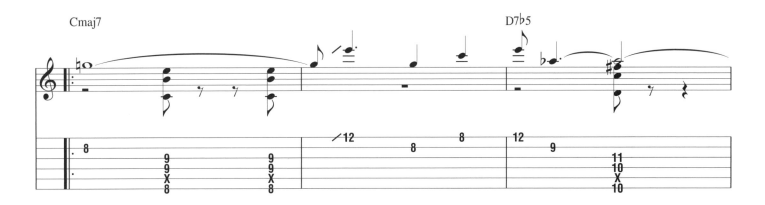

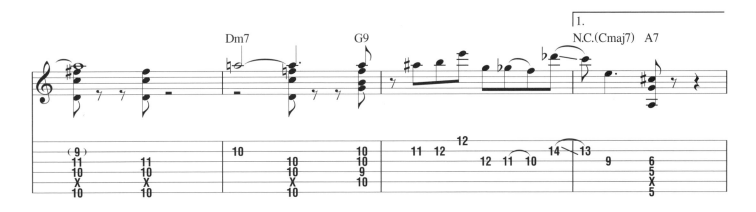

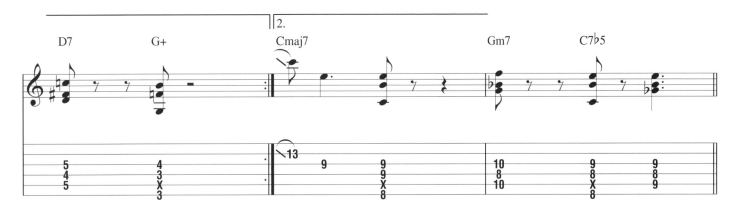

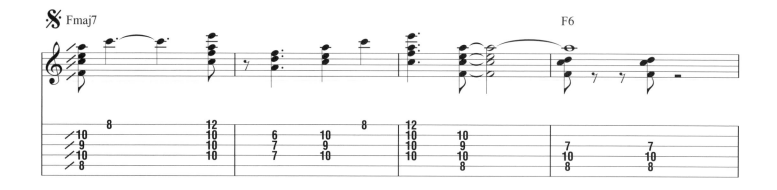

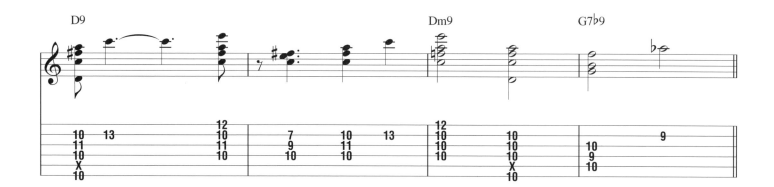

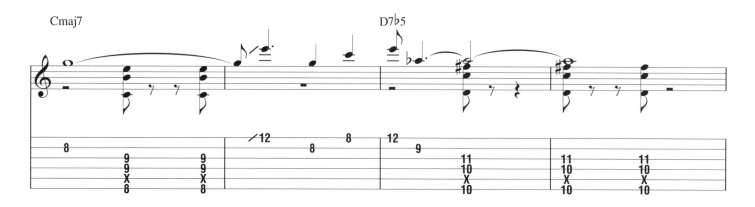

To Coda ⊕

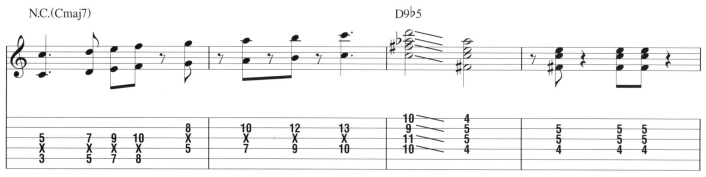

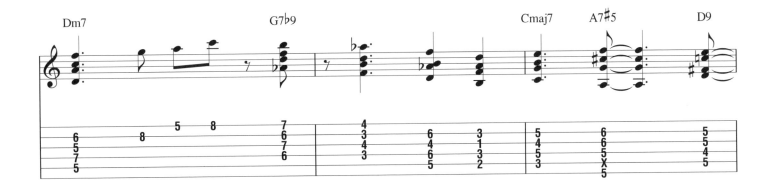

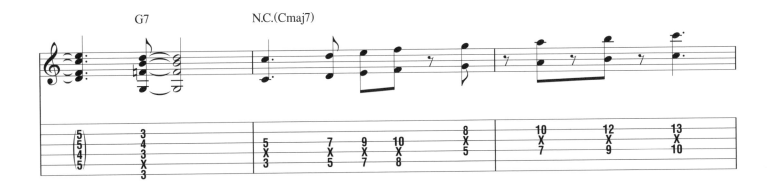

D.S. al Coda

This Masquerade

Words and Music by Leon Russell

Moderately slow

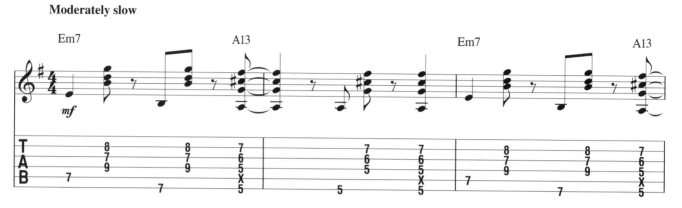

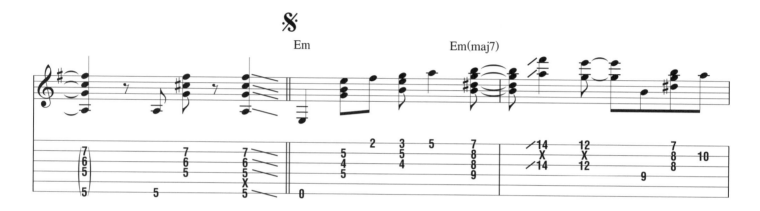

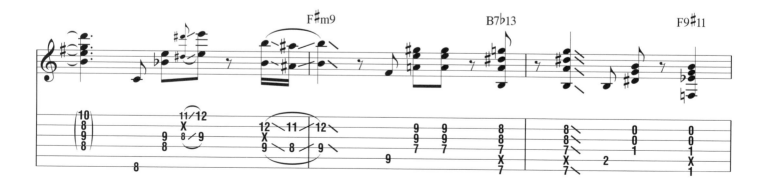

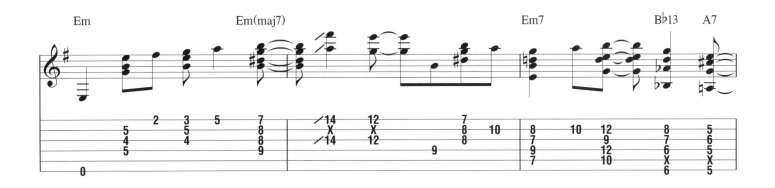

To Coda ⊕

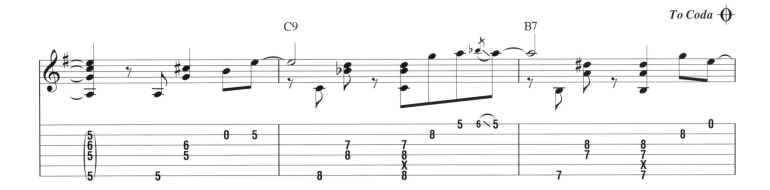

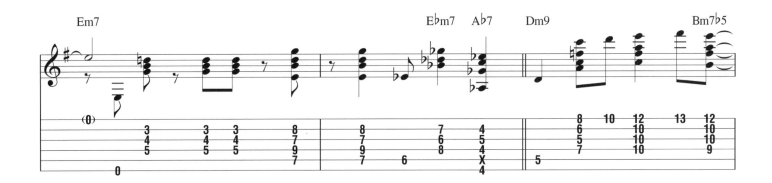

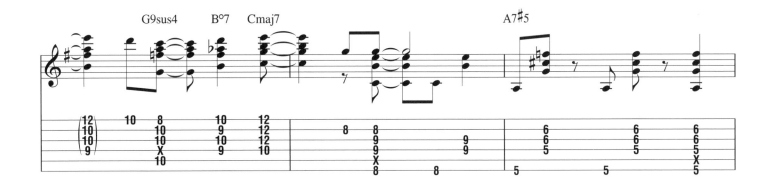

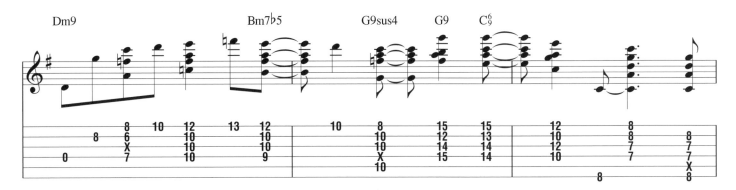

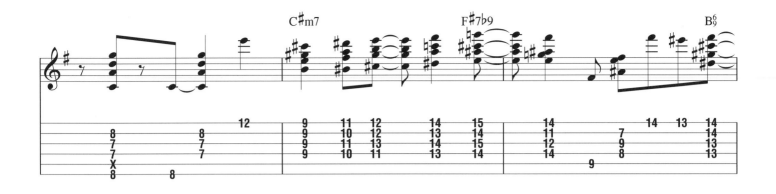

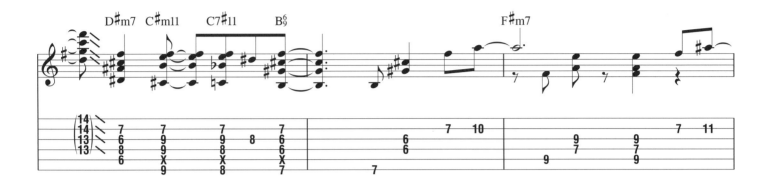

D.S. al Coda

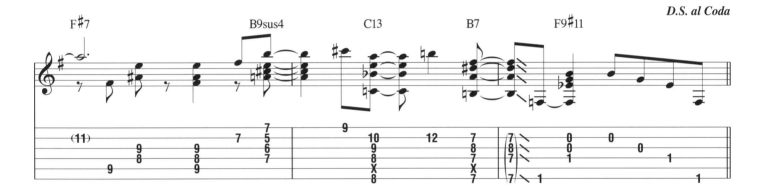

Coda

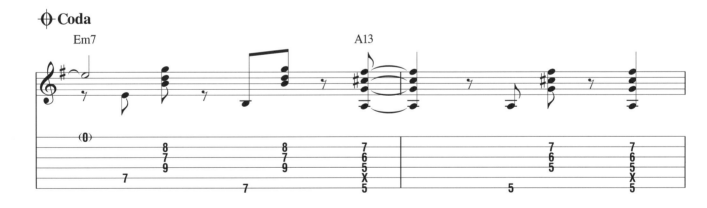

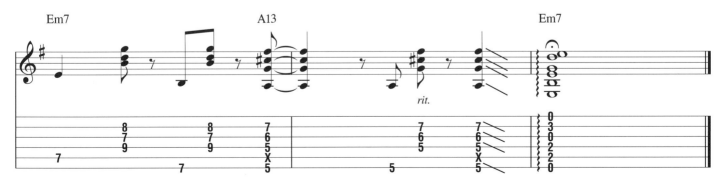

GREAT STEELY DAN BOOKS

 *from* **CHERRY LANE MUSIC COMPANY**

STEELY DAN'S GREATEST SONGS
15 more trademark Steely Dan songs, including: Aja • Chain Lightning • Daddy Don't Live in That New York City No More • Everyone's Gone to the Movies • Haitian Divorce • Josie • Pretzel Logic • Reeling in the Years • and more.
02500168 Play-It-Like-It-Is Guitar $19.95

BEST OF STEELY DAN FOR SOLO GUITAR
11 great solos, including: Aja • Babylon Sisters • Deacon Blues • Doctor Wu • Gaucho • Haitian Divorce • Hey Nineteen • Kid Charlemagne • Peg • Rikki Don't Lose That Number • Third World Man.
02500169 Solo Guitar..$12.95

BEST OF STEELY DAN FOR DRUMS
10 classic songs for drums from Steely Dan. Includes: Aja • Babylon Sisters • The Fez • Peg • Two Against Nature • Time Out of Mind • What a Shame About Me • and more.
02500312 Drums $18.95

STEELY DAN LEGENDARY LICKS (GUITAR)
28 extensive musical examples from: Aja • Babylon Sisters • Black Cow • Bodhisattva • Josie • Kid Charlemagne • Parker's Band • Peg • Reeling in the Years • Rikki Don't Lose That Number • and many more.
02500160 Guitar Book/CD Pack...$19.95

STEELY DAN JUST THE RIFFS FOR GUITAR
by Rich Zurkowski
More than 40 hot licks from Steely Dan. Includes: Babylon Sisters • Black Friday • The Boston Rag • Deacon Blues • Kid Charlemagne • King of the World • Peg • Reeling in the Years • Rikki Don't Lose That Number • Sign in Stranger • and more.
02500159 Just the Riffs – Guitar..$19.95

THE ART OF STEELY DAN (KEYBOARD)
Features over 30 great Steely Dan tunes for piano: Aja • Black Cow • Bodhisattva • Hey Nineteen • I.G.Y. (What a Beautiful World) • Parker's Band • Reeling in the Years • Third World Man • Your Gold Teeth II • many more.
02500171 Piano Solo $19.95

STEELY DAN JUST THE RIFFS FOR KEYBOARD
28 keyboard riffs, including: Babylon Sisters • The Boston Rag • Deacon Blues • Don't Take Me Alive • Green Earrings • Hey Nineteen • Peg • Reeling in the Years • Rikki Don't Lose That Number • and more.
02500164 Just the Riffs – Keyboard $9.95

BEST OF STEELY DAN
A fantastic collection of 15 hits showcasing the sophistocated sounds of Steely Dan. Includes: Babylon Sisters • Bad Sneakers • Deacon Blues • Do It Again • FM • Here at the Western World • Hey Nineteen • I.G.Y. (What a Beautiful World) • Josie • Kid Charlemagne • My Old School • Peg • Reeling in the Years • Rikki Don't Lose That Number • Time out of Mind.
02500165 Piano/Vocal/Guitar $14.95

STEELY DAN – ANTHOLOGY
A comprehensive collection of 30 of their biggest hits, including: Aja • Big Noise, New York • Black Cow • Black Friday • Bodhisattva • Deacon Blues • Do It Again • Everyone's Gone to the Movies • FM • Gaucho • Hey Nineteen • Josie • Reeling in the Years • more!
02500166 Piano/Vocal/Guitar $17.95

BEST OF STEELY DAN FOR GUITAR
15 transcriptions of Steely Dan's jazz/rock tunes, including: Bad Sneakers • Black Friday • The Boston Rag • Deacon Blues • FM • Green Earrings • Kid Charlemagne • Parker's Band • Peg • Rikki Don't Lose That Number • Third World Man • Time Out of Mind • and more.
02500167 Play-It-Like-It-Is Guitar $19.95

Prices, contents, and availability subject to change without notice.

CHERRY LANE MUSIC COMPANY
6 East 32nd Street, New York, NY 10016

EXCLUSIVELY DISTRIBUTED BY
HAL•LEONARD® CORPORATION
7777 W. BLUEMOUND RD. P.O. BOX 13819 MILWAUKEE, WI 53213

http://www.halleonard.com

0401